COMPOSER
SHOWCASE
HAL LEONARD
STUDENT PIANO LIBRARY

INTERMEDIATE/LATE INTERMEDIATE LEVEL

Romantic Expressions

FIVE PIECES FOR PIANO SOLO

BY CAROL KLOSE

ISBN 978-1-4768-0521-4

HAL•LEONARD®
CORPORATION

7777 W. BLUEMOUND RD. P.O. BOX 13819 MILWAUKEE, WI 53213

In Australia Contact:
Hal Leonard Australia Pty. Ltd.
4 Lentara Court
Cheltenham, Victoria, 3192 Australia
Email: ausadmin@halleonard.com.au

Visit Hal Leonard Online at
www.halleonard.com

CONTENTS

Performance Notes

In composing the five pieces in this book, I had very definite imagery in mind, and chose "forms" from the Romantic era in which to couch those images and musical ideas.

There are two facets to the performance of each composition:

- First, evoking the **imagery** expressed in the main title through interpretation.
- Second, keeping in mind the style of the **form** indicated in the subtitle.

The combined set offers a wide variety of moods, tempi, and performance techniques that I hope are appealing to both the performer and listener. These Intermediate/Late Intermediate pieces make a fine introduction to traditional Romantic repertoire. One might even hear a glimpse of a particular composer or two from the past in these Romantic styles...

I would like to thank Linda Kennedy for commissioning "A River's Tale," which is dedicated to her and her students. I would also like to thank my editor, Jennifer Linn, for her constant encouragement and support.

I dedicate this book to the memory of my dear husband John.

—Carol Klose

Cuckoo at Twilight
(Album Leaf)

Albumblatt, the German word for "album leaf," was a title given to many short descriptive pieces in the Romantic era. I like to picture this piece as a little sketch of a cuckoo in someone's long-lost musical "album."

In this piece, one hears the familiar, plaintive song of the cuckoo—two RH notes in a simple descending third (D-B). This motive follows the melodic phrases like a commentary heard in a forest at the end of the day. The changing light of the coming evening is reflected by the addition of the sometimes unstable LH accompaniment notes—the major 7th on E-D♯, for example—that weave in and out of the G Major harmony present in the RH melodic phrases.

- To achieve the proper effect, the LH should be played very quietly, to blend in with and support the *legato* RH melody rather than accentuate the dissonances produced by the LH D♯'s.
- The second note of the LH two-note slurs should always be played with a soft, gentle touch.
- With the A1 section, starting at meas. 18, the LH accompaniment is played an octave lower, resulting in a fuller sound. The LH melody should be played more boldly in meas. 27-30, gradually resolving to a quiet feel that ends with the Coda in meas. 41-48.

Imagine the whole scene disappearing in the misty night at the end, punctuated by the sweet faint song of the cuckoo.

If I Were a Dove
(Nocturne)

In this piece one can hear the influence of the Chopin nocturnes in the *cantabile* melodic phrases, soft LH accompaniment, melismatic *gruppetti*, grace note figures, and variation in the repeat of melodic lines. For this reason, "If I Were a Dove" would be a useful preparatory piece for the traditional nocturne repertoire.

As I composed this piece, I imagined what it would feel like to be a dove—elegantly gliding and soaring through the air, bringing its promise of peace. In particular, the RH ascending lines in meas. 63-74 bear this imagery. It is important to carry the gracefulness of the dove into the performance, creating a calmness through the RH grace notes and rhythmic variations. Note that the LH accompaniment pattern in the A and A1 sections is repeated over and over, giving the RH freedom to blend the rhythms and melodic shapes with ease.

- In the LH accompaniment in the A sections, play with a heavy arm, arching from the elbow to make a gentle leap between the bass notes and the intervals on beats 2 and 3 in each measure. This will help the LH hand avoid unwanted accents.
- Always bring out the RH melody, shaping each phrase with *cresc.* and *decresc.* and releasing with a relaxed wrist.
- Play grace notes ahead of the beat.
- For the seven-note *gruppetto* in meas. 18, use the *rit.* to play gently and evenly to beat 1 in meas. 19.
- To execute the wide intervals in the LH accompaniment in meas. 19-50, keep the hand rounded, playing on the corner of the thumb and using a light touch for thumb notes.
- In meas. 41-44, bring out the countermelody indicated by the LH *tenuto* marks.

- For the trill in meas. 49-50, begin on B (B-C-B-C etc.), and taper off to a slower tempo, so the last note of the trill (C) leads smoothly to the first note (B) of meas. 51.
- In meas. 71, depress the LH F octave slowly to avoid a harsh sound. Follow with a sudden *decresc.* and *rit.* to the end. Imagine the dove flying away with the ascending parallel 6ths in this final passage.

Gypsy Fire
(Rhapsody)

What better musical way to express extreme moods and quick attitude changes than in a "rhapsody?" This name was popular in the Romantic era to describe pieces in which the music poured forth in emotion from the heart—perfect for telling an exciting musical story.

"Gypsy Fire" is in the style of a Hungarian rhapsody, filled with extremes of emotion and passion. There are many changes in dynamics and tempi in this piece, and the changes are often quick and always contrasting. One should exaggerate all the articulations and expression marks, becoming an actor onstage for this flashy piece.

- The opening measures should be played with great energy that tapers off with the rit. in meas. 4. This should be followed by a complete break (//) before going on to the andante theme.
- Meas. 7-14 are very expressive and require a *rubato* feel.
- The triplet pickup notes in the next section should be played boldly and not too fast, setting a strong beat for the measures to come.
- At meas. 20, there should be a complete break before the last sixteenth note E-natural.
- Because of the many changes between triplet and duplet rhythms, it is important to keep track of the main beats, playing the groups evenly in between evenly. Saying "trip-le-it" (for triplets) and "huck-le-ber-ry" (for four sixteenth notes) can be helpful when counting.
- It is important to keep the articulations and pedaling exact, as they help define the attitude changes in this piece.
- The final three chords should be played fast, with crisp staccatos and accents to create the final explosion in this "Gypsy Fire."

A River's Tale
(Arabesque)
(Commissioned by the Piano Studio of Linda Kennedy, Maumelle, Arkansas)

The flowing "arabesque" style seems just right to musically describe a river. In this piece, the river is the Arkansas, a long watery thoroughfare that passes through Little Rock, bearing with it traces of history—as a home to Native American Indian tribes, a passageway to the west for settlers, a transport on the Trail of Tears, a waterway carrying steamboat trade, to its present-day system including man-made locks.

The form of this piece is A B A1 Coda, with "A" depicting the flowing water. The shift in keys from A Major to F♯ minor (meas. 21) helps describe a darker side of the river traffic, as the Arkansas played a role in the transport of Native American Indians on the Trail of Tears. The image created by the RH two-note slurs in the Coda (meas. 55-58) is one of a boat moored at the shore, rocking gently with the lapping wavelets.

- Use full arm weight to control evenness and dynamic flow, especially in the arpeggiated passages, playing on the corner of the thumb rather than the side.
- Keep the arms heavy but free to move from position to position throughout the piece.
- At meas. 21, bring out the top RH notes for a strong melody supported by a steady but subdued LH rhythm.
- At meas. 55 change to a calmer, slower tempo. Lean into RH beat 1 for the two-note slurs to recreate a "rocking" motion.
- At meas. 59, play the RH as a soft accompaniment figure, while the LH shapes the melodic line through meas. 61.

The Hills of Glamorgan
(Ballade)

The musical term "ballade" describes a piece that is often both lyrical and that tells a story—qualities I had in mind for this composition.

Glamorgan is the southernmost county in Wales, Great Britain. Its varied scenery includes hills, vales, and mountains that border the northern shores of the Bristol Sea. It is an area I have visited often, and that holds many memories for me. In this piece I wanted to capture the feel of its present-day beauty as well as strains of the ancient Celtic culture that is such a part of the hardy Welsh nature.

The A section consists of a lyrical folk-like melody, contrasted with a lilting dance in 6/8 time in the B section, concluding with a return to the lyricism of the A section. Both the Intro and Coda in "The Hills of Glamorgan" are reminiscent of church bells ringing over the hills, quaint villages and mining towns of the area.

- When the meter changes from 2/2 to 2/4 in meas. 4 and 65, the half-note beat becomes the quarter-note beat from that point on.
- Play the first statement of the theme in the A section (meas. 9-22) freely, as if singing a tender ballad.
- The second time the melody is heard, (meas. 23) the sixteenth-note accompaniment patterns add more rhythmic foundation, but continue to maintain a *rubato* feel.
- Articulate the RH grace notes in meas. 30 and 39 gently, but play the sixteenth-dotted eighth patterns in meas. 13, 20 and 38 with a "bite."
- Keep a lilting "2" feel in the B section in 6/8 time.
- After the *rit.* and held arpeggiated chord in meas. 56, return immediately to the lively accented tempo of the previous measures, which then transition calmly to A1.
- In meas. 63, the dotted quarter note becomes the half-note beat for 2/2.
- In the Coda (meas. 89-92), roll the arpeggiated bell chords and use the *una corda* pedal so the sound gradually fades to nothing.

Cuckoo at Twilight

(Album Leaf)

By Carol Klose

Plaintively (♩ = 120)

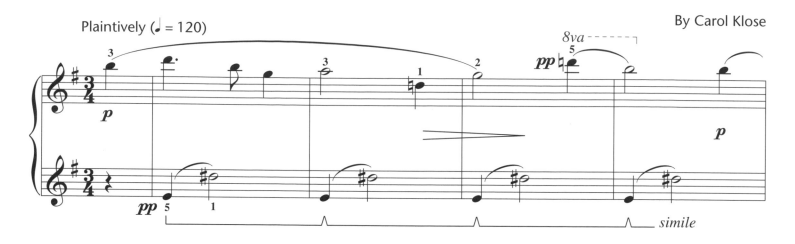

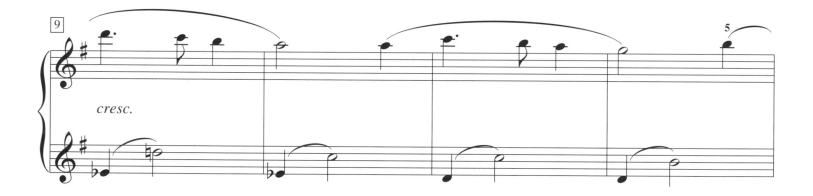

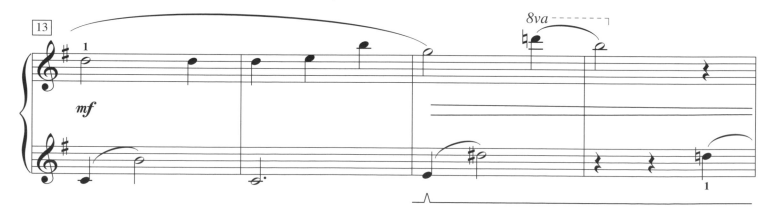

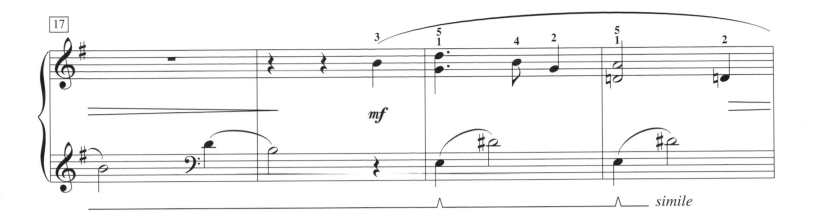

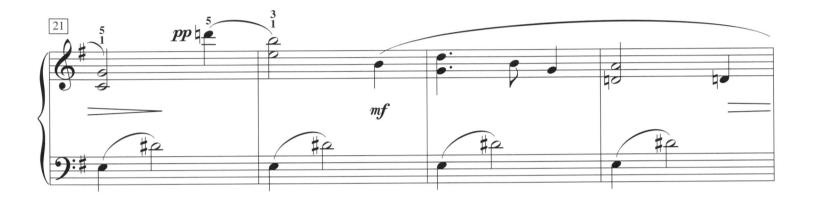

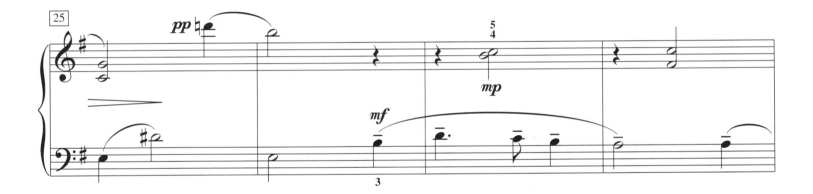

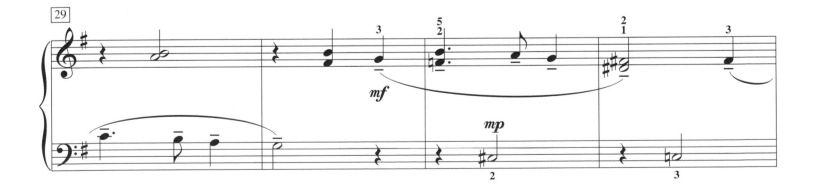

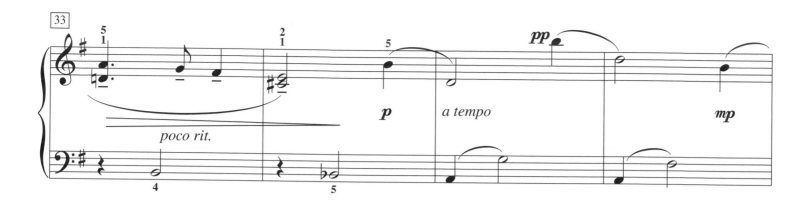

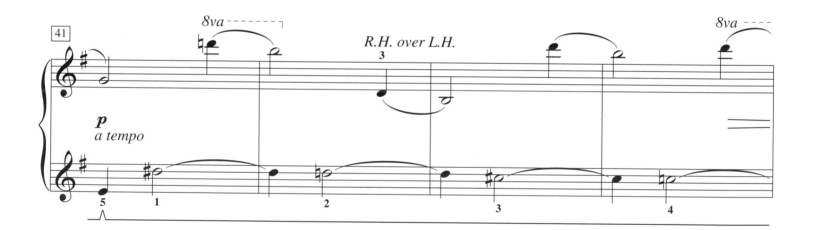

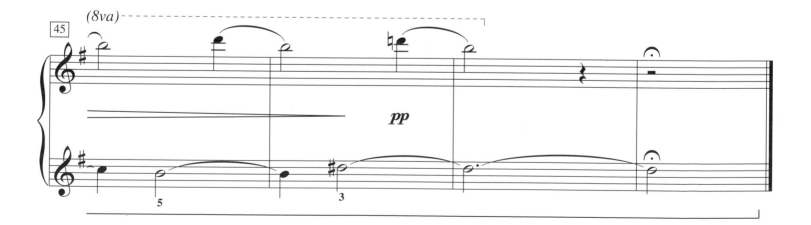

If I Were a Dove

(Nocturne)

By Carol Klose

Andante espressivo (♩ = c. 80)

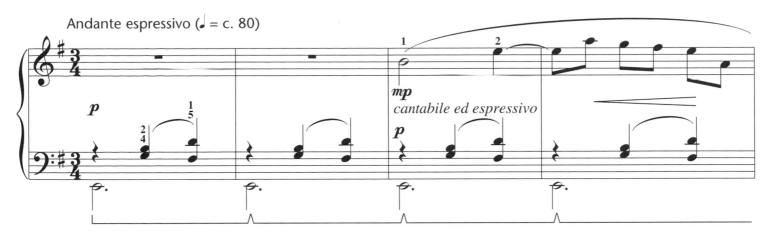

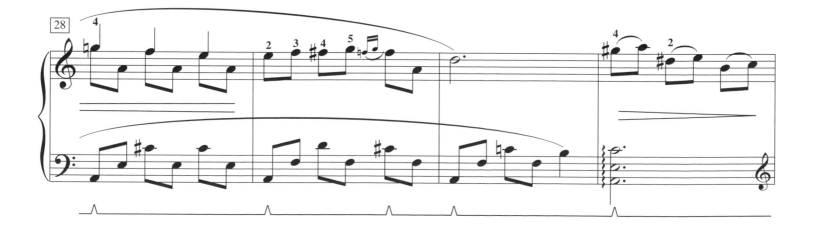

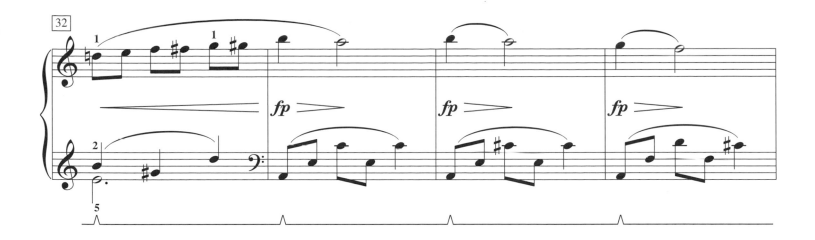

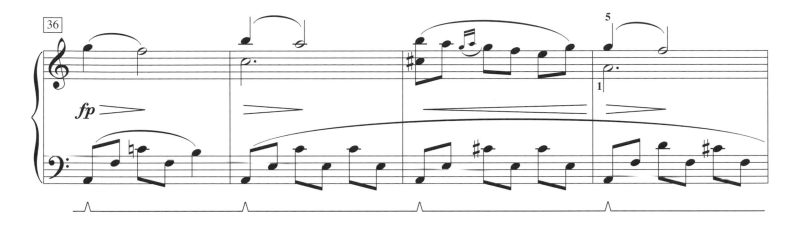

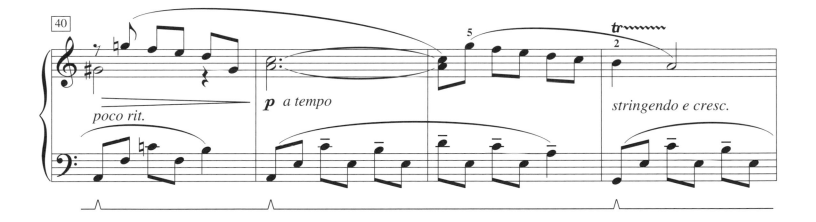

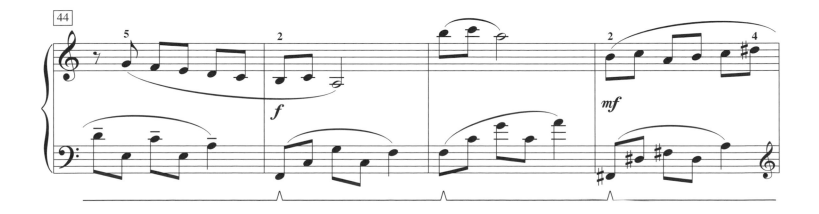

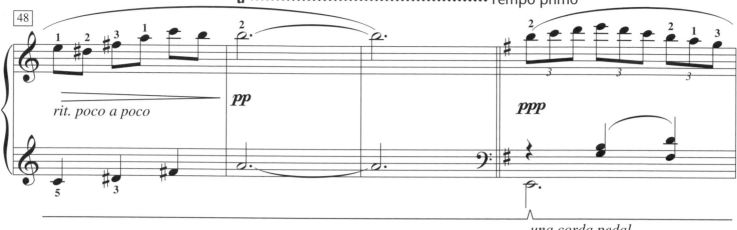

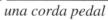

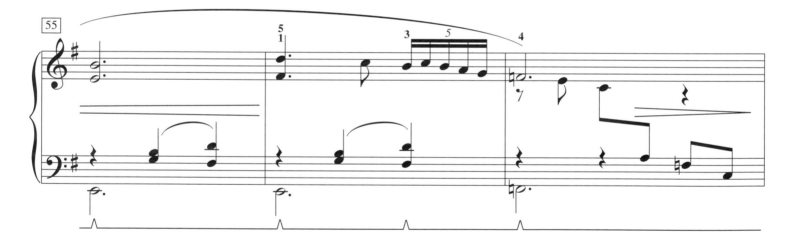

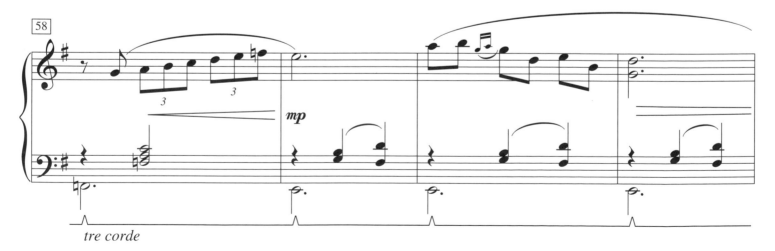

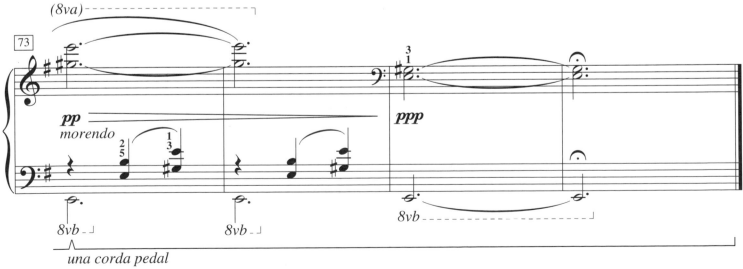

Gypsy Fire

(Rhapsody)

By Carol Klose

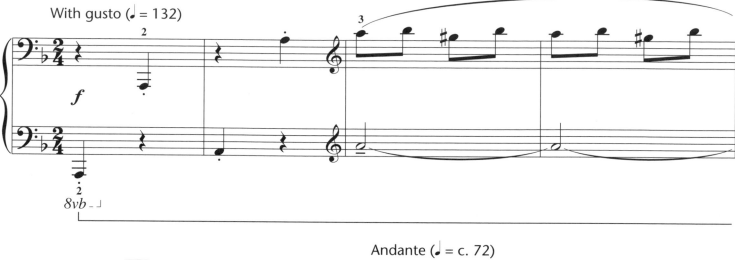

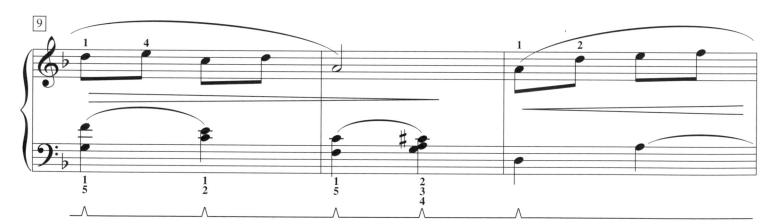

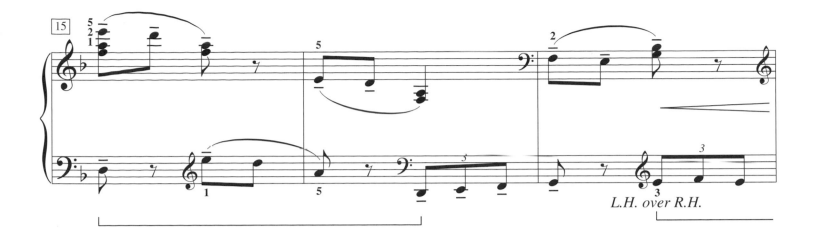

Boldly and steadily (♩ = 84)

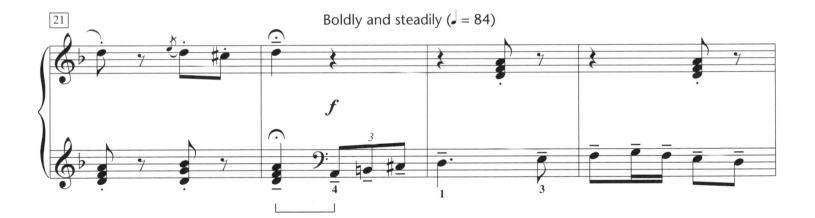

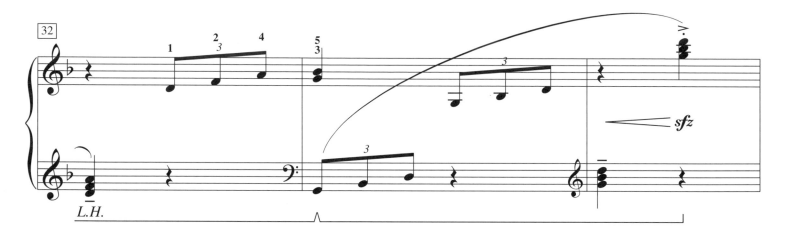

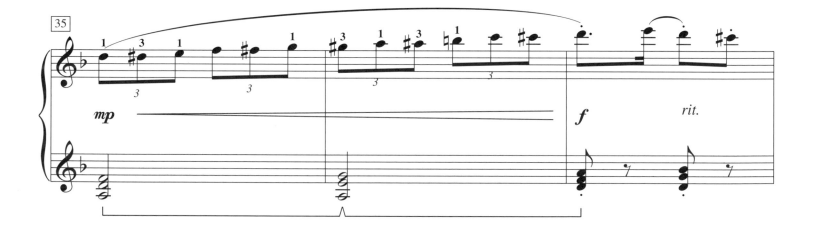

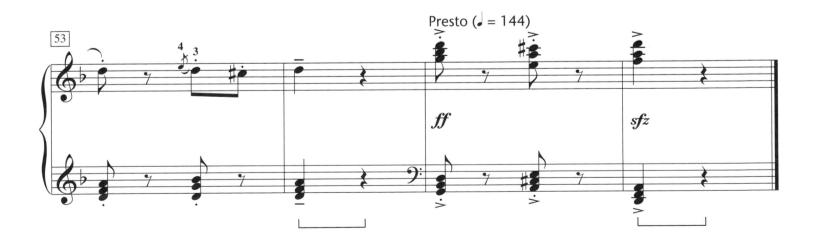

19

The Hills of Glamorgan
(Ballade)

By Carol Klose

Moderately, in 2 (♩ = 76)

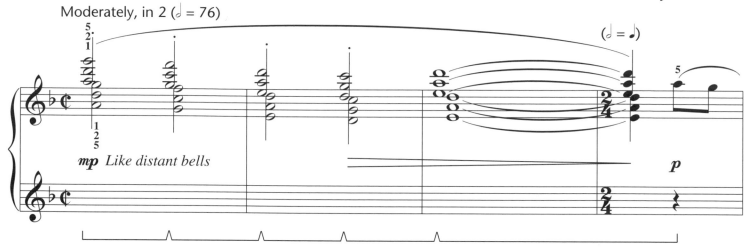

mp Like distant bells

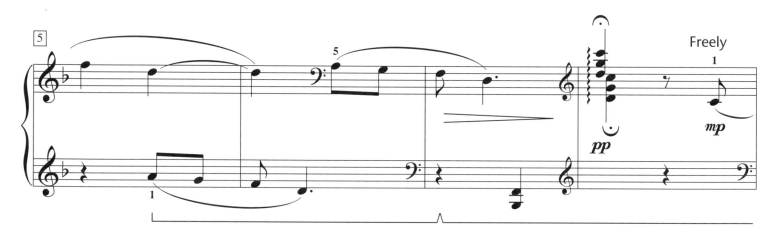

Freely

espressivo

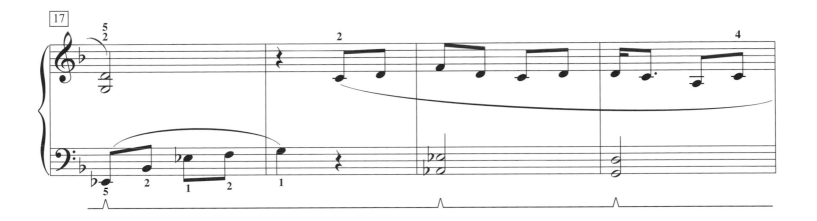

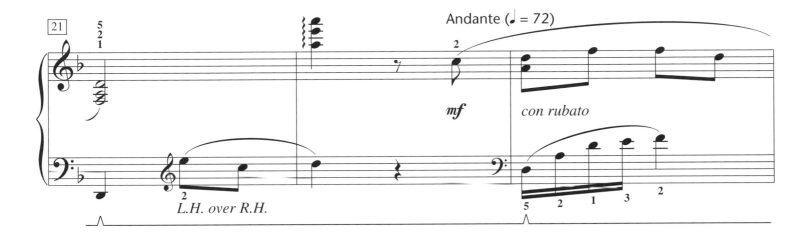

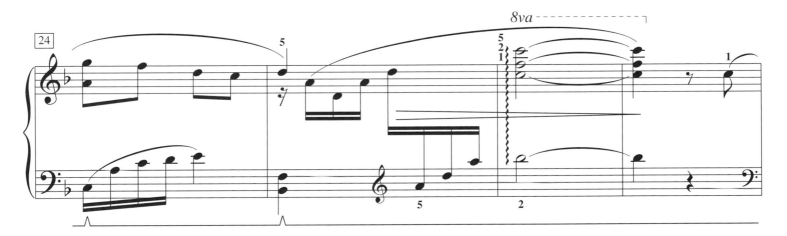

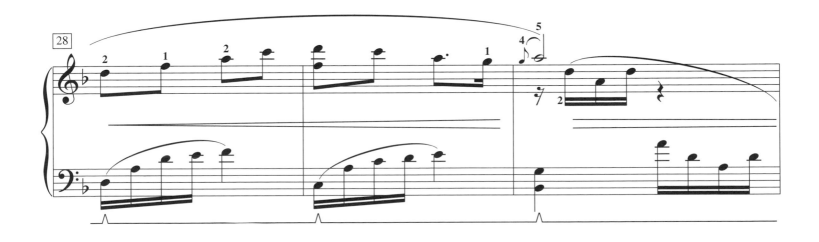

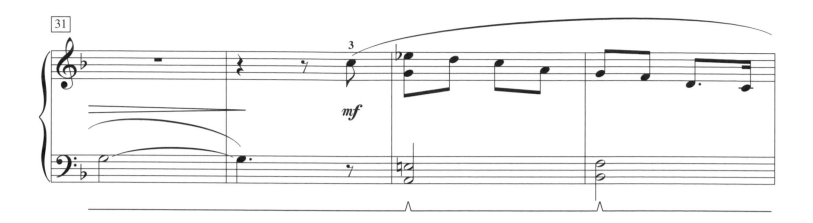

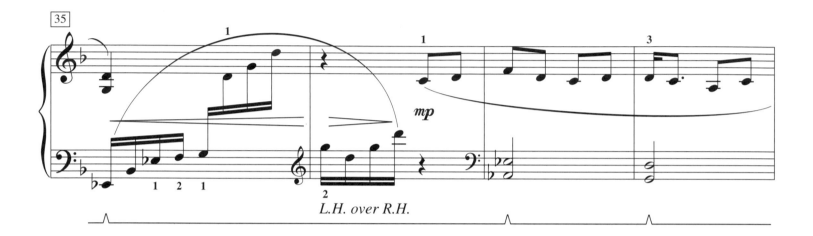

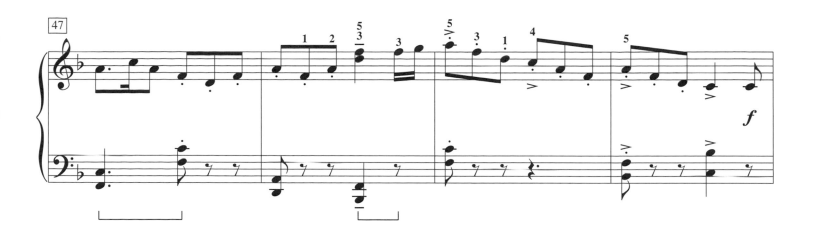

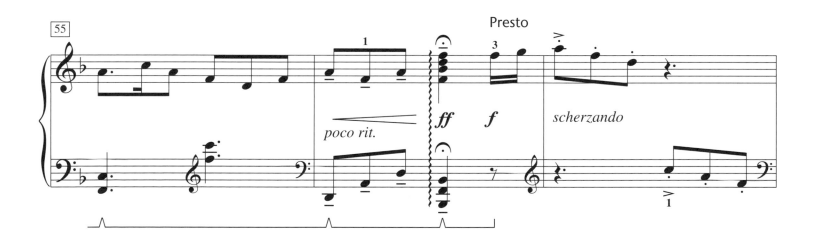

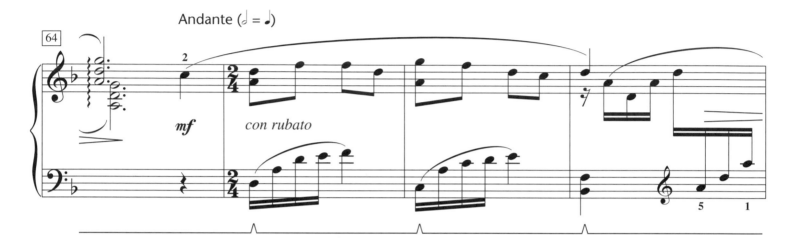

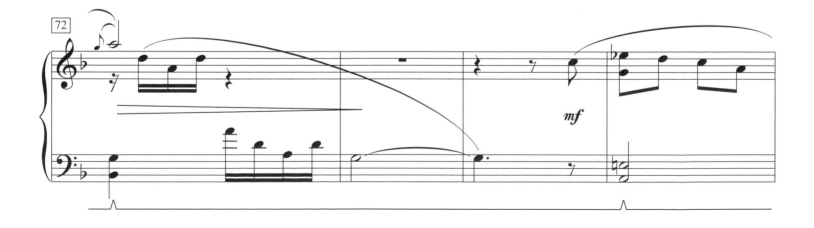

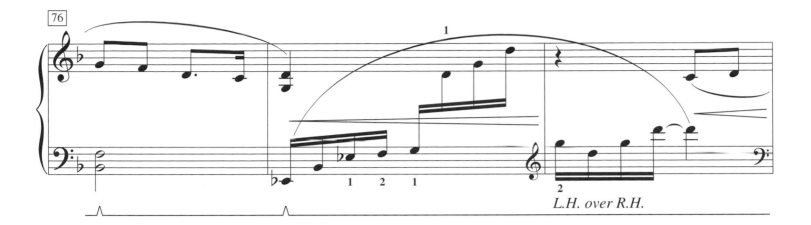

L.H. over R.H.

pp

mp

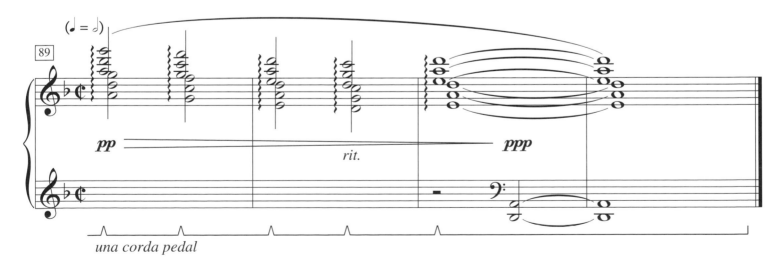

pp

rit.

ppp

una corda pedal

25

A River's Tale
(Arabesque)

Commissioned by the Piano Studio of Linda Kennedy, Maumelle, Arkansas

By Carol Klose

Flowing, in 2 (♩ = 72)

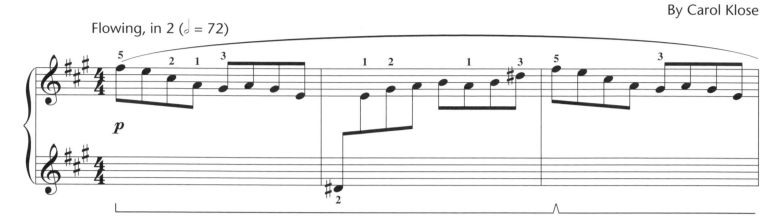

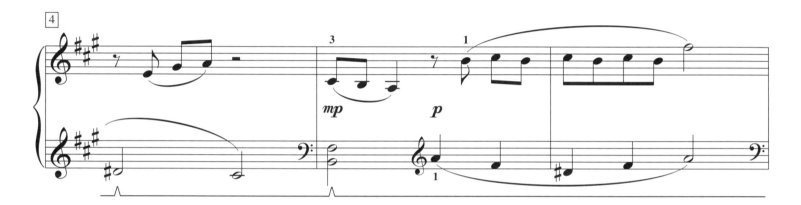

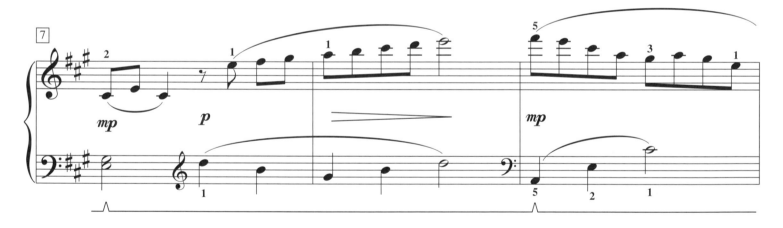

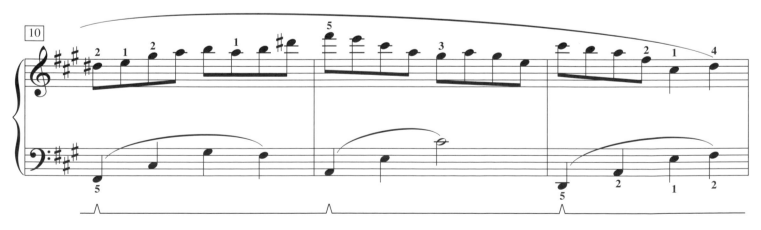

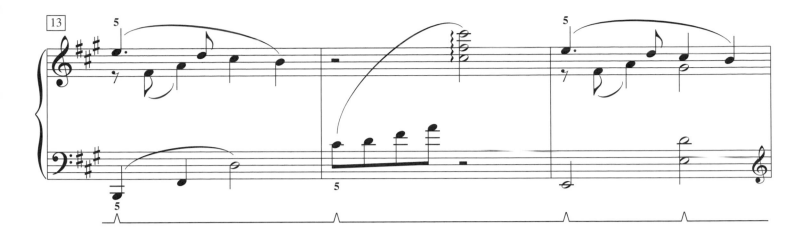

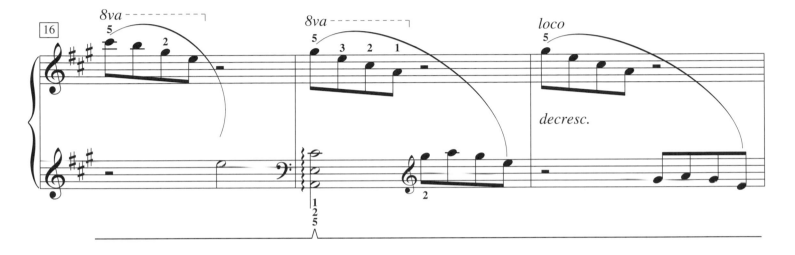

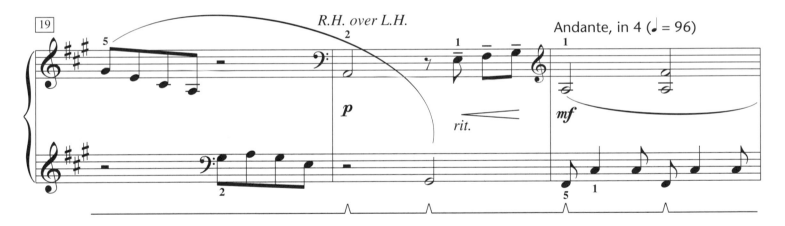

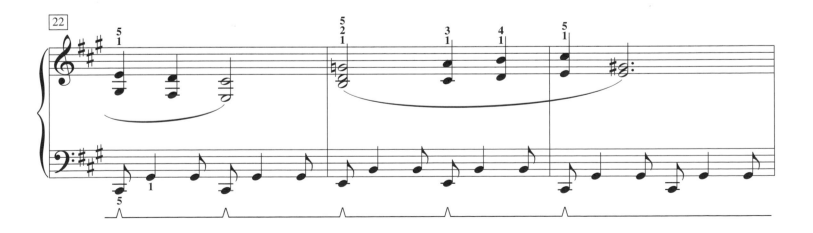

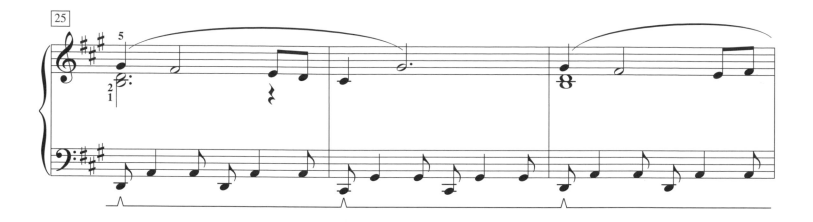

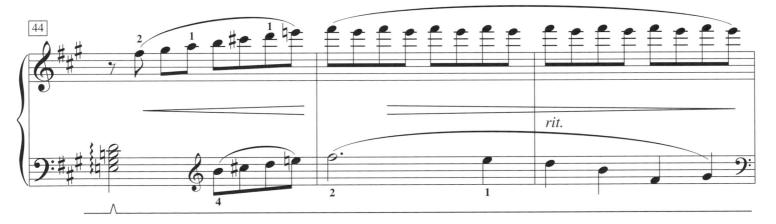

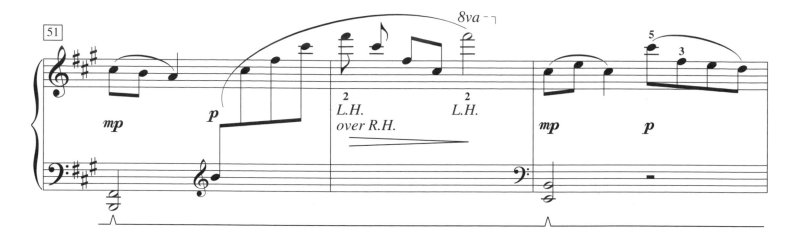

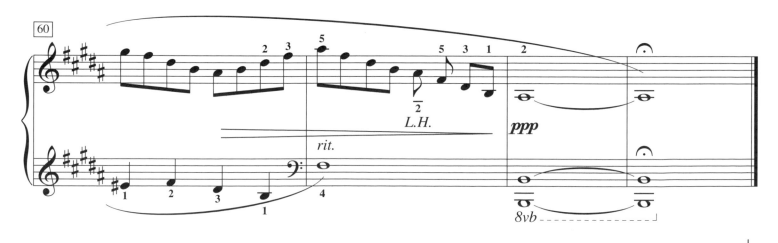

COMPOSER SHOWCASE
HAL LEONARD STUDENT PIANO LIBRARY

This series showcases great original piano music from our **Hal Leonard Student Piano Library** family of composers, including Bill Boyd, Phillip Keveren, Carol Klose, Jennifer Linn, Mona Rejino, Eugénie Rocherolle and more. Carefully graded for easy selection, each book contains gems that are certain to become tomorrow's classics!

BILL BOYD

JAZZ BITS (AND PIECES)
Early Intermediate Level
00290312 11 Solos......$6.99

JAZZ DELIGHTS
Intermediate Level
00240435 11 Solos......$7.99

JAZZ FEST
Intermediate Level
00240436 10 Solos......$7.99

JAZZ PRELIMS
Early Elementary Level
00290032 12 Solos......$6.99

JAZZ SKETCHES
Intermediate Level
00220001 8 Solos......$6.99

JAZZ STARTERS
Elementary Level
00290425 10 Solos......$6.99

JAZZ STARTERS II
Late Elementary Level
00290434 11 Solos......$7.99

JAZZ STARTERS III
Late Elementary Level
00290465 12 Solos......$7.99

THINK JAZZ!
Early Intermediate Level
00290417 Method Book......$10.99

TONY CARAMIA

JAZZ MOODS
Intermediate Level
00296728 8 Solos......$6.95

SUITE DREAMS
Intermediate Level
00296775 4 Solos......$6.99

SONDRA CLARK

DAKOTA DAYS
Intermediate Level
00296521 5 Solos......$6.95

FAVORITE CAROLS FOR TWO
Intermediate Level
00296530 5 Duets......$7.99

FLORIDA FANTASY SUITE
Intermediate Level
00296766 3 Duets......$7.95

ISLAND DELIGHTS
Intermediate Level
00296666 4 Solos......$6.95

THREE ODD METERS
Intermediate Level
00296472 3 Duets......$6.95

MATTHEW EDWARDS

CONCERTO FOR YOUNG PIANISTS
FOR 2 PIANOS, FOUR HANDS
Intermediate Level Book/CD
00296356 3 Movements......$16.95

CONCERTO NO. 2 IN G MAJOR
FOR 2 PIANOS, 4 HANDS
Intermediate Level Book/CD
00296670 3 Movements......$16.95

PHILLIP KEVEREN

MOUSE ON A MIRROR
Late Elementary Level
00296361 5 Solos......$6.95

MUSICAL MOODS
Elementary/Late Elementary Level
00296714 7 Solos......$5.95

ROMP! – BOOK/CD PACK
A DIGITAL KEYBOARD ENSEMBLE FOR SIX PLAYERS
Intermediate Level
00296549 Book/CD......$9.95
00296548 Book/GM Disk......$9.95

SHIFTY-EYED BLUES
Late Elementary Level
00296374 5 Solos......$6.99

TEX-MEX REX
Late Elementary Level
00296353 6 Solos......$5.95

CAROL KLOSE

CORAL REEF SUITE
Late Elementary Level
00296354 7 Solos......$6.99

DESERT SUITE
Intermediate Level
00296667 6 Solos......$7.99

FANCIFUL WALTZES
Early Intermediate Level
00296473 5 Solos......$7.95

GARDEN TREASURES
Late Intermediate Level
00296787 5 Solos......$7.99

TRADITIONAL CAROLS FOR TWO
Late Elementary Level
00296557 5 Duets......$7.99

WATERCOLOR MINIATURES
Early Intermediate Level
00296848 7 Solos......$7.99

JENNIFER LINN

AMERICAN IMPRESSIONS
Intermediate Level
00296471 6 Solos......$7.99

CHRISTMAS IMPRESSIONS
Intermediate Level
00296706 8 Solos......$6.99

JUST PINK
Elementary Level
00296722 9 Solos......$6.99

LES PETITES IMAGES
Late Elementary Level
00296664 7 Solos......$7.99

LES PETITES IMPRESSIONS
Intermediate Level
00296355 6 Solos......$7.99

REFLECTIONS
Late Intermediate Level
00296843 5 Solos......$7.99

FOR MORE INFORMATION, SEE YOUR LOCAL MUSIC DEALER,
OR WRITE TO:

HAL•LEONARD®
CORPORATION
7777 W. BLUEMOUND RD. P.O. BOX 13819 MILWAUKEE, WI 53213

For full descriptions and song lists for the books listed here, and to view a complete list of titles in this series, please visit our website at www.halleonard.com

TALES OF MYSTERY
Intermediate Level
00296769 6 Solos......$7.99

MONA REJINO

CIRCUS SUITE
Late Elementary Level
00296665 5 Solos......$5.95

JUST FOR KIDS
Elementary Level
00296840 8 Solos......$7.99

MERRY CHRISTMAS MEDLEYS
Intermediate Level
00296799 5 Solos......$7.99

PORTRAITS IN STYLE
Early Intermediate Level
00296507 6 Solos......$7.99

EUGÉNIE ROCHEROLLE

JAMBALAYA
FOR 2 PIANOS, 8 HANDS
Intermediate Level
00296654 Piano Ensemble......$9.99

JAMBALAYA
FOR 2 PIANOS, 4 HANDS
Intermediate Level
00296725 Piano Duo (2 Pianos)......$7.95

TOUR FOR TWO
Late Elementary Level
00296832 6 Duets......$7.99

CHRISTOS TSITSAROS

DANCES FROM AROUND THE WORLD
Early Intermediate Level
00296688 7 Solos......$6.95

POETIC MOMENTS
Intermediate Level
00296403 8 Solos......$7.95

SONATINA HUMORESQUE
Late Intermediate Level
00296772 3 Movements......$6.99

SONGS WITHOUT WORDS
Intermediate Level
00296506 9 Solos......$7.95

THROUGHOUT THE YEAR
Late Elementary Level
00296723 12 Duets......$6.95

ADDITIONAL COLLECTIONS

AMERICAN PORTRAITS
by Wendy Stevens
Intermediate Level
00296817 6 Solos......$7.99

**MONDAY'S CHILD
(A CHILD'S BLESSINGS)**
by Deborah Brady
Intermediate Level
00296373 7 Solos......$6.95

PLAY THE BLUES!
by Luann Carman (Method Book)
Early Intermediate Level
00296357 10 Solos......$8.99

PUPPY DOG TALES
by Deborah Brady
Elementary Level
00296718 5 Solos......$6.95

WORLD GEMS
FOR 2 PIANOS, 8 HANDS
arr. by Amy O'Grady
Early Intermediate Level
00296505 6 Folk Songs......$6.95

Piano Recital Showcase

"What should my students play for the recital?" This series provides easy answers to this common question. For these winning collections, we've carefully selected some of the most popular and effective pieces from the **Hal Leonard Student Library** – from early-elementary to late-intermediate levels. You'll love the variety of musical styles found in each book.

PIANO RECITAL SHOWCASE PRE-STAFF
Pre-Staff Early Elementary Level
8 solos: Bumper Cars • Cherokee Lullaby • Fire Dance • The Hungry Spider • On a Magic Carpet • One, Two, Three • Pickled Pepper Polka • Pumpkin Song.
00296784 .... $6.99

BOOK 1
Elementary Level
12 solos: B.B.'s Boogie • In My Dreams • Japanese Garden • Jazz Jig • Joyful Bells • Lost Treasure • Monster March • Ocean Breezes • Party Cat Parade • Rainy Day Play • Sledding Fun • Veggie Song.
00296749 .... $7.99

BOOK 2
Late-Elementary Level
12 solos: Angelfish Arabesque • The Brontosaurus Bop • From the Land of Make-Believe • Ghosts of a Sunken Pirate Ship • The Happy Walrus • Harvest Dance • Hummingbird (L'oiseau-mouche) • Little Bird • Quick Spin in a Fast Car • Shifty-Eyed Blues • The Snake Charmer • Soft Shoe Shuffle.
00296748 .... $7.99

BOOK 3
Intermediate Level
10 solos: Castilian Dreamer • Dreaming Song • Jump Around Rag • Little Mazurka • Meaghan's Melody • Mountain Splendor • Seaside Stride • Snap to It! • Too Cool to Fool • Wizard's Wish.
00296747 .... $7.99

BOOK 4
Late-Intermediate Level
8 solos: Berceuse for Janey • Cafe Waltz • Forever in My Heart • Indigo Bay • Salsa Picante • Sassy Samba • Skater's Dream • Twilight on the Lake.
00296746 .... $7.95

CHRISTMAS EVE SOLOS
Intermediate Level
Composed for the intermediate level student, these pieces provide fresh and substantial repertoire for students not quite ready for advanced piano literature. Includes: Auld Lang Syne • Bring a Torch, Jeannette, Isabella • Coventry Carol • O Little Town of Bethlehem • Silent Night • We Wish You a Merry Christmas • and more.
00296877 .... $8.99

DUET FAVORITES
Intermediate Level
Five original duets for one piano, four hands from top composers Phillip Keveren, Eugénie Rocherolle, Sondra Clark and Wendy Stevens. Includes: Angel Falls • Crescent City Connection • Prime Time • A Wind of Promise • Yearning.
00296898 .... $9.99

ROMANTIC INSPIRATIONS
Early Advanced Level
From "Arabesque" to "Nocturne" to "Rapsodie," the inspired pieces in this collection are a perfect choice for students who want to play beautiful, expressive and impressive literature at the recital. Includes: Arabesque • Journey's End • Nocturne • Nocturne d'Esprit • Prelude No. 1 • Rapsodie • Rondo Capriccioso • Valse d'Automne.
00296813 .... $8.99

SUMMERTIME FUN
Elementary Level
Twelve terrific originals from favorite HLSPL composers, all at the elementary level. Songs: Accidental Wizard • Butterflies and Rainbows • Chill Out! • Down by the Lake • The Enchanted Mermaid • Gone Fishin' • The Merry Merry-Go-Round • Missing You • Pink Lemonade • Rockin' the Boat • Teeter-Totter • Wind Chimes.
00296831 .... $7.99

Visit our website at **www.halleonard.com/hlspl.jsp**
for all the newest titles in this series and other books
in the Hal Leonard Student Piano Library.

Prices, content, and availability subject to change without notice.

NORMAN DELLO JOIO

SUITE FOR PIANO

G. SCHIRMER, Inc.

DISTRIBUTED BY